THE END OF POVERTY

THE END OF POVERTY

AUGUST RAINES

CONTENTS

CHAPTER 1

Introduction to Poverty and Sustainable Development

"The End of Poverty" was written by Jeffrey Sachs in 2005. The book presents a plan to eradicate extreme global poverty through sustainable development and international cooperation. It was a New York Times bestseller. The author gives his analysis based on twenty-five years of financial experience and historical data. Divided into ten chapters, the book's main focus is on the strategies necessary to help poor countries make the transition from destitution to sustainable economic growth. In each of these strategies, Sachs provides valuable and timely insights and points the direction to finding solutions to material poverty. The book is a summary of Sachs's lectures at Columbia University to various public policy officials and opinion makers.

Sachs was the head of the United Nations Millennium Project, whose work underpinned the eight Millennium Development Goals, which if achieved would reduce global poverty significantly by the year 2015. Much of the information in "The End of Poverty" comes from the project, which started in 2002 and ran until 2005. Sachs shows convincingly that we have the resources to end poverty, if only the rich world, maligned as it is, would commit to providing those resources. In this book, he gives us a rare chance to be inspired to attack a global problem which is underscored by volitional malnutrition, infectious and parasitic diseases, unmanageable debt, and a fatal lack of annual and seasonal income security.

Defining Poverty and Sustainable Development

First, let me do a quick review of what extreme poverty is, how we define it and how extreme is extreme. Second, I would ask what we mean by the so-called new rule and what would be sustainable development. That is going to be the new rule. It is something, of course, that has not yet become the prevailing assumption or policy rule. Third, what are the key initiatives or strategies consistent with this new rule? What should we be looking at? What should we be addressing if the idea gets implemented into economic policies? Fourth, what are the institutions specific global ways to assure that we move ahead in the right direction in ending extreme poverty around the world? That's the subjects to which I hope to address in the remarks.

I want to thank the organizers of this conference for inviting me and making it possible for me to share ideas about what I consider to be the most important or fundamental topic, certainly the most fundamental topic among economic issues today: how to end poverty in the world. Over the past one or two years, I think that the awareness that extreme poverty can be ended, must be ended, has been rising at a rapid pace. It is an idea whose time has clearly come. The clergy has for many years been speaking loudly and much more persuasively than economists about the nearly 25,000 deaths per day from extreme poverty. There is, I believe, the general awareness that extreme poverty is not a consequence of personal failure on the part of those caught in the poverty trap.

Historical Overview of Poverty

But not everyone shared in these resources. Modern poverty appeared, and recent studies have shown that it is rising. Compared to the general living conditions of the average American, there are now groups experiencing levels, durations, and probabilities of poverty that are qualitatively and quantitatively different. The number of people living below this comfortable threshold is relatively modest. But if we lower the limit to families experiencing levels of destitution considered unacceptable for the citizens of a rich nation, the proportion of poverty jumps to 14 percent of the population. Lowered even further to a level where poverty is obvious and almost unbearable - poor people with a total family income more than 50 percent less than the average relative poverty line – 33 percent of Americans find themselves among the poor. From the time of the U.S. Declaration of Independence to the opening of the twentieth century, the United States presented the best opportunity for progress and well-being. Then came the New Frontier, a country and a people that seemed indestructible. By the end of the century, the concept of the New World conjured up images of poverty and inequality that were scarcely imaginable. The frontier was rich, but in its shadow lay an underdeveloped country that was poor. Economic progress depends on many things, and, foremost, on keeping the peace and an absence of civil wars. Once again, some people see a development spiral operating with other forces that make it possible to escape from history. The main obstacles of poverty are obvious: land distribution, population growth, education, and more equitable salaries.

Historical Overview of Poverty in Wealthy Nations: The two waves of industrialization in the nineteenth and twentieth centuries produced enormous economic progress. In 1800, the majority of the people in the world lived mainly in the countryside, employed in agriculture. Over the next 80 years, a fantastic population shift then took place, from the country to the city. In 1870, 58 percent of the American population was rural, while in 1930, 56 percent of Americans lived in urban centers. Poverty accompanied the extraordinary economic expansion; the new urban labor market seemed to create a parallel labor market. It could absorb the working force, but completely excluded the minority of people who could not demonstrate their ability or willingness to work. In 1873, Carl Menger established that there is a minimum income that a worker absolutely must have if he or she is to survive. At the end of the nineteenth century, Alfred Marshall estimated that a family called "to live a healthy life" needed no less than £1.44 a week. At the time, one-fifth of the British working class was living on less than this amount. In the United States in the 1950s, we saw the beginning of a new economic model – "Fordism" - which offered a relatively high level of salaries and fair working conditions, including access to decent housing. Overproduction was managed through advances in social protection, such as pensions, unemployment, and health insurance. This system had a long life, up until the oil shock of 1973. After that date, the Fordist pact gradually eroded, resulting in the government's decision to gradually liberalize its economy. Although the causes are mixed, efficiency and production considerably increased.

Grasping the meaning of poverty is not easy. To do so requires an understanding of a country's economic and social system, as well as an understanding of individual, regional, and national situations. The study of poverty also involves the examination of the social structure, governance, state policies, and the specific role of each individual and his or her position in society.

Importance of Sustainable Development in Poverty Alleviation

As stated by the United Nations, sustainable development must meet the needs of the present without compromising the ability of future generations to meet their own needs. It means maintaining the necessary balance between the goals of poverty alleviation and economic development and the safeguarding of natural resources and the environment. In addition, it means finding solutions that are both economically and socially viable and, at the same time, environmentally sound. Sustainable development means that the needs of the present are met without jeopardizing the capacity of future generations to meet their own needs. The concept of sustainable development calls for a combination of strategies that pursue economic and social development goals, while sustaining the resource base and the environment for future generations.

Sustainable development is essential for poverty alleviation and for overall socio-economic development. If sustainability is not given priority, efforts to achieve poverty reduction and economic growth will not last. Despite increasing awareness of the importance of the environment, environmental problems continue to grow and their effects continue to be felt. It is not possible to alleviate poverty amid declining natural resources and environmental conditions since poverty and natural resource and environmental problems are closely linked. Even in the face of a poor and deteriorating environment, the poor themselves are the ones who are left to deal with environmental problems.

CHAPTER 2

Globalization and Poverty

The developing world has never had as good an opportunity to end global poverty as it has today. The opportunity is good because of globalization. Never have the developing countries of the world been as involved in the global economy as they are today. Never has there been as much international trade and as many financial flows as today. Travel has never been as easy, and communication has never been so open and so great. For many, the fascination with globalization is that workers can now live wherever wages are highest, companies can produce wherever it is cheapest and sell goods wherever the demand is greatest, governments face pressures to attract labor and capital by lowering taxes and reducing trade restrictions, and there is a powerful process underway that is beginning the equalization of the wages of workers worldwide. This report discusses how to sustain this momentum that brings opportunity and hope to the world's poorest.

Globalization is a process of integration that results from increasing human, economic, social, and cultural exchange. Globalization in this sense binds the world more closely together through exchange in trade, finance, technology, and both ideas and culture. This is in contrast to international trade that is similarly intended to bind the developing and developed worlds more closely together, and which is a closely related aspect of globalization in many respects, but is not as broad and does not to the same extent require standardizing taxes, regulation and reform in developing nations, or integrating the world's poor into the global economy. The evidence suggests that globalization in the broader sense of that word has had, and is having, a powerful effect in lifting tens of millions of people out of extreme poverty since at least the early 1980s. This report is about ways to make certain that these new opportunities that are opening to so many more people persist, that they multiply, and that they extend to all of the world's regions and nations.

Impact of Globalization on Poverty

It is evident then, that trade is not an end in itself; trade must be made to favor the reduction of the discipline. The increases in productivity, in fact, do not necessarily derive from a policy expressive of the favor; they are a consequence of the demand advantage of the favorable factors.

But the key question is: How must those who govern the countries to the South think about the defense of the employment of their own people? They must pay attention to the promotion of employment and integration in globalization, open labor markets, basic education, and primary health care of the best quality, and also pensions, when one no longer works because one is old or sick. In the prevention of poverty, these are the basic pillars of the Social State.

It becomes manifest, then, that small rural producers in EDCs are broadly called to compete with farmers in the countries of the North, where the practice of massive protection is in force. The support for agriculture, which the OECD countries have established to safeguard their national farmers from the dangers inherent in an activity indispensable for the collective, is reduced to the area of the per acre "box". This box can contain help for climatic difficulties, support for mechanization, expenses for straw and animal building materials, as well as contributions to investments in farm relation structures.

In general, the defense of the labor market through a contraction of social rights is the better strategy for lower unemployment. With this in mind, when social rights are reduced in Emerging and Developing Countries (EDCs), the consequence is an increase in unemployment and a higher labor market pressure on wages.

Globalization, the process of increased integration among countries, primarily aims to enable worldwide exchange of goods and services. Most often, it is characterized by both advanced technologies as well as investments. International trade and investment, representing the current direction of the clearly deterministic economic policies, favor large firms and this principle applies likewise to both sectors, namely agriculture and industry. This situation forces peasants and laborers of the poorer countries to give away their work for remuneration deflated by an expedited openness of their markets, where insufficient regulations do not assure the existence of a welfare state.

Debates on the Relationship between Globalization and Poverty
Whilst the former perspective was adhered by the Chartist and American movements of workers originating in the early industrialization, and of trade unions, the latter was defended by the classical economies, such as David Ricardo, Adam Smith, John Stuart Mill, who wrote in favor of the possibility to promote dependency relations and solidarities between workers concerning a greater industrial progress. As the nineteenth century debate, the last years of the present century are characterized by a series of controversies on the relationship between globalization and income inequality. How-

ever, such relation is more complex if confronted with the matter of poverty.

The recent rise of anti-globalization protests in rich countries raises fundamental questions about the social implications of globalization. While some labor groups and developing countries suggest that the benefits of globalization can be high and widely shared, others contend that globalization deeply benefits the rich to the detriment of the poor and will further polarize the world and increase poverty. The debate about globalization has mirrored a similar debate widespread during the nineteenth century on the connection between international trade and poverty. This proliferated in the confrontation of two opposite beliefs, of which one observed an association between trade adversities and heightened income inequality, whilst the other associated trade with higher wages and lower inequality.

CHAPTER 3

Economic Strategies for Poverty Reduction

Education is one of the most fundamental and universally beneficial investments that can be made in people and expands the abilities of the poor to improve their own lives. It enables boys and girls to achieve their individual potential and is a key technology of development. Additionally, macroeconomic policies can either induce or help prevent poverty reductions. It is always the case that some poor will grow richer through their own efforts, but the process can be facilitated by sound policies and implemented by effective institutions. A key element of the successful country strategies of the future will be higher and pro-poor growth. Country strategies for higher and pro-poor growth surely will be diverse. Nevertheless, there are several economic factors that have almost universally benefited the cause of poverty reduction. It is neither necessary nor realistic that all of these should exist for economic development to take place. In the specific case of China, the Chinese transformation has been most unusual but has greatly reduced world poverty and underscored the potential economic impact of the world's poorest people.

Though poverty is a multidimensional problem that extends beyond income measures, the core of the problem is about money. Investment in the poor is the first and most fundamental of economic strategies. People indeed are the most important asset of a nation. Investments in health, nutrition, and education build human capacities and are vital for the long-term success of economic development and poverty reduction. Investments can also be direct, for example, to create an appropriate environment for private business and to sound infrastructure or social safety nets. Experience all over the world demonstrates that proposals to somehow reduce poverty based on some sort of magical formula that bypasses needed investments in the poor simply do not work.

Microfinance and Small Business Development

One successful alternative to the provision of funds is that of the Grameen Bank. This rural-based, non-profit institution specializes in microfinancing. Its unique mechanism for helping individuals invest in their future is in its ability to lend money to borrowers without traditional forms of collateral and at a very low rate of interest. In the case of the Grameen Bank, the average financial cost to their clients is 1.44 percent per month. Therefore, as total assets accumulate, so does an overall standard of living. When more money is saved, it can be invested either into current operations or used as a cushion against emergency expenses.

The reality is that many small and microenterprises lack access to credit or face interest rates of 10 to 20 percent per month. Many households that lack access to credit are forced to sell their labor to others simply to meet day-to-day expenses. The members of the household are often separated from one another on a daily basis. Microentrepreneurs could have the potential to expand their enterprises if given some start-up funds to purchase flour, machinery, etc.

The primary problem with the provision of formal credit markets arises because small and microenterprises usually lack collateral.

Investment in Education and Skills Training

The high costs of education - direct costs such as tuition, fees, and the cost of uniforms and books, as well as opportunity costs of student earnings, transporting students to and from school, and other costs can be insurmountable hurdles for poor families. Government provision of free education or stipends to poor families to offset the costs of primary education are two methods of assisting families in sending their children to school.

The evidence suggests that governments play a crucial role in promoting and financing primary education. In most countries, it is virtually impossible for poor or uneducated families to pay for their children's primary education without governmental assistance. Not only are poor families unable to afford it, often they are unwilling to sacrifice the opportunity costs associated with keeping their children at home. Many parents feel that child labor, though it may have negative long-term effects, is an essential way of alleviating family poverty in the short-term and do not wish to solely bear the costs of immediate benefit upon their own children.

Agricultural Development and Food Security

If the objective of improving food distribution is to improve food consumption by the poor, interventions aimed at the demand side of the malnourishment problem have been shown to be more effective than those with a supply side focus. Cash transfer programs targeted to mothers with malnourished children, conditional on their actively participating in a nutrition education program, report quite significant improvements in child health. Moreover, even if there are missing markets for credit, it is much less clear that there is market failure which will keep children from being fed.

Rural poverty rates are exceedingly high in most countries - five times higher than urban poverty rates, on average. In more than twenty "strategic countries", rural populations number more than one third of the total population. A great majority of these countries have an underdeveloped and heavily subsistence agricultural sector, where high levels of poverty are manifest. Even in countries where large urban populations depend on commercial farmers in the rural areas for their food supply, however, less than 20 percent of all food spending will be on the farm. The striking evidence of the fact that most food is produced by small farmers has significant implications for strategies to reduce poverty and accelerate growth. Furthermore, most malnourished children in developing countries live in rural areas.

CHAPTER 4

Social Strategies for Poverty Alleviation

The poor are the most affected by the lack of basic health care, nutrition, and education that affects not only the present but the long-run capabilities of all who survive into adulthood. More fundamentally, human dignity and self-esteem demand more than certain levels of individual well-being as measured by per capita income. They depend on all this but also on the respect of the fundamental rights of independence of the persons who form the basis for social life, and on the respect of the natural and social environment. It is very simple-mindedly foolish indeed to ignore the fact that the poor will survive and are indeed trying to survive and have the basic social infrastructure to help them achieve what other human beings - from the most affluent to the ethanol workshop participant - want and need.

When only the private provision of these services is considered, the poor are excluded, but the targeted implementation of these policies can ensure that the poor will not be excluded, that they will benefit directly from the collective consumption provided by the implementation process. Thus, the logical implication of considering increasing returns in services is to seriously consider the possibility of direct social strategies - poverty alleviation strategies - that promote the provision of these services and price all goods and services at social marginal cost, including proper remuneration for their social reproduction. The success of these strategies should be measured not only by the improvement of the conditions of the poor but also by the realization of these increasing returns in the delivery of social services. Not only do these targeted strategies ensure that the poor participate, but success actually implies the incorporation and positive feedback effects. The poor are the most vulnerable to the most dangerous infectious diseases. They are also the most sensitive and are usually most directly affected by environmental degradation. They are the first ones to suffer when affordable but efficient preventive and curative services provided to others are not assured.

Healthcare and Sanitation Programs

Sanitation is the primary focus of the largest investments in rural infrastructure that a village district will make in a typical year. In practice, this low-level equilibrium arises when the poor live cheek by jowl without adequate sanitation, and because of the neglect by the poor of their children's health, health continues to be a binding constraint to the poor having higher human capital. A household's allocation of household labor and other resources to the care of sick children and the money cost to the household of the care of sick children both increase as more children in the household become ill at the same time. These negative externalities help to keep the poor in the low-level equilibrium. District-wide water-type sanitation programs as key elements in their development strategy are discussed.

While relatively large expenditures on health infrastructure will benefit the poor, they will mostly benefit the better off in low-income countries. It is the programs that are specifically targeted to the poor that will result in improved health outcomes for the poor.

A promising approach is an urban medical program where public health clinics, located close to the poor, are amply stocked and provide free medical care. Preventive medical vaccination campaigns against diseases such as diphtheria, tetanus, whooping cough, measles, and polio, to be effective, must cover the vast majority of the nation's population. National programs of free oral rehydration therapy education are also seen as being helpful, particularly when a nation's adult illiteracy rate is relatively low.

Gender Equality and Women's Empowerment

Investment in health, education, and empowerment of women also plays a key role in human development, that precious commodity of good politics in an age teetering on the brink of religious wars. On all three, we can show important gains when public policy can identify resulting in high return, leaving all preconceived notions aside. In terms of social spending, secondary and tertiary education shows the highest rate of return, not just for increased earnings but also for improvements in women's health, fertility and child survival, all of which help to reduce poverty. For women, health matters mostly for the welfare of others. When resources are scarce, men spend a higher proportion of their increased earning on themselves, women invest in the human capital of future generation, unlocking the potential of future growth. Women, therefore, make hidden selfless investments in basic health and education, the most crucial of special public goods-making reduced budget oppressive a source of relief to individuals and governments alike. And donors should be no exception: always ask "how do women and children at doing?" when the record of your social/current spending falls short of your lofty goals.

When women are fully involved, the benefits can be seen immediately: families are healthier and better fed; their income, savings, and reinvestment go up. And what is true in micro is true in macro. The surest way to help the billions of women struggling to move from the margins to the mainstream of the global economy is, in fact, to accelerate the globalization process. An educated, empowered woman has the sixth sense in the emerging global economy. So, she makes a natural entrepreneur, naturally caring for family and community. But her active participation is partly blocked by public policy - paid and unpaid policies. And it is partly blocked by tradition and practice. There are many people with noble goals of trying to work it down. But how do we make a breakthrough in speed and broadness?

Community Development Initiatives

Sustainable community economic development is a major element in building the capacity of poor communities to benefit from their participation in the global economy. Because the benefits of enterprise growth and employment generation have been limited to certain areas within the developing world and to certain people within those areas, the International Labour Organization as well as the United Nations and a number of national development agencies have placed added emphasis on programs to assist both the urban and rural poor to improve their living standards through the stimulation of small and medium-sized enterprises. There is a growing realization that both the design and application of development intervention, in particular, by promoting the demand-orientation of government agencies, promoting social dialogue as a means to adjust employment and enterprise development to changes in the external and internal economic environments, and promoting enterprise and skills sector development, can make a significant contribution to addressing the social and economic problems of communities and individuals, whatever the economic and social development status of the country in which they live.

CHAPTER 5

Environmental Sustainability and Poverty Reduction

Given the difficulties encountered in estimating both income and price elasticities of damaging emissions, we do not know exactly the root causes of the rapid growth of environmental damage during the industrial revolution. Although no one disputes that the modern cash economy devastated existing institutions and diets, it is unlikely that this harmful effect depended substantially on levels of per capita income. The discovery of sewage-crusted antiquities in 4,000-year-old Crete revives the question of why advanced ancient cities failed to grow pollution-free. They may have had no reason to adopt pollution-free living practices.

This chapter attempts to answer four questions: Why have many environmental indicators deteriorated as countries become richer? What are the economic consequences of environmental policy? What policy instruments do we have to address environmental externalities? After describing the brief history of industrial pollution, we address the central question of the chapter: How is it that as countries become richer the window between income and environmental quality first deteriorates and then improves? We then address the question of the poor as victims of environment, here pollution from industrial and transport centres. We are now ready to discuss the main question of this paper: If the direction of causation runs from environmental quality to poor outcomes, how can we find diseases of affluence while poor people are still dependent upon polluted water?

Climate Change Adaptation and Mitigation

Policymakers need to be aware of the potential impacts of both climate change and their adaptation and mitigation policies on poverty. Given limited public resources, protecting poor communities from the impacts of climate change poses a challenge. On the one hand, development of clean technologies is hampered by public sector failures that do not encourage choice of optimal long-term strategies. On the other hand, developing adaptation to the impacts of climate change might be the optimal long-term strategy for some locations. The development policies of the international community also have the potential to significantly alter adaptive capacity. The specific impacts depend upon the specifics of the climate change and development policies associated with it.

It is widely recognized that global climate change presents a clear and present danger to our collective future. The increase in the frequency and severity of extreme climatic events in recent years raises serious questions about the potential impacts of climate change, particularly for vulnerability and adaptation to those impacts. The issue of climate change has been framed as a development issue, including the identification of linkages with poverty reduction policies and sustainable development. The urgency with which climate change requires action has called for implementation of mitigation measures, the integration of considerations on climate change in the funding sources channeled through the multilateral development banks and other international agencies, and increasing awareness on the potential impacts of climate change on poor communities dependent on natural resources. Central questions in this debate are for whom and how can climate change contribute to sustainable development.

Renewable Energy and Access to Clean Water

The main areas where renewable energy sources are currently employed on a significant scale are in power generation and in heating the water that provides space heating and sanitation needs. In the U.S., water heating ranks second only to space heating as a primary energy consumer in the residential sector, with 89% of homes heated by hot water tank or tankless heater. Because heat pumps require less electricity than the low efficiency of resistance heaters, a shift from resistance heating to heat pump heating can result in a decrease of associated greenhouse gas emissions, even accounting for the additional power used. In either electric resistance heating or electric heat pump households, water heating is often an important secondary service provided by the electrical grid. Consequently, if water heating was to be provided through alternative off-grid methods, the demand from the grid for both services could be reduced, stranding some of the existing investment in overcapitalized infrastructure.

In many developing countries, people who are not connected to the electrical grid have virtually no chance of raising their income to international poverty levels. That is why expanded access to electricity is perhaps the single most important objective that can be pursued in raising incomes for the poorest. A critical medium-term step to make this increased energy use more sustainable is to increase the proportion of energy produced from renewable sources. While many environmental and developmental co-benefits are generated from increased reliance on renewable energy sources, high first-cost to produce is often incurred relative to conventional sources.

CHAPTER 6

Political Stability and Governance in Poverty Alle

But as the world shifts its focus from previously taken-for-granted issues like security and income distribution toward "state capacity" or "governance", it is in many ways recognizing that enhancing the efficiency and fairness of public institutions is a central challenge. Perceptions about a lack of "good governance" are listed as key factors underlying the decline in the living standards of many African countries and the rise of regional disparities in living standards elsewhere. Furthermore, to the extent that defining an appropriate role for public agencies and then selectively working to strengthen them could be an important part of poverty reduction strategies, part of the larger issues of societal values, transaction costs and politics need to be faced. The question is how the concern about "governance" and state capacity can be translated into practical action. And of course political systems embody group interests; who or what it is that generates and implements policy depends a lot on how political interests are organized and how state organizations themselves are structured. Nurturing more effective policy action is not an easy process; getting the analysis and the institutional design wrong can lead in undesirable directions. Simply stated, the task is to make policy work better, not to pretend that there are universal practices appropriate to all times and places. So the real challenge for poverty alleviation is not the need for "good policies" in the abstract. It is the need for appropriate policy strategies and successful state organizations that respond to the unique situations of the poor.

Recent discussions of the causes of long-term growth and development success or failure have emphasized the importance of appropriate policy and institutional environments as prime determinants of relatively good development outcomes. That formulations of political and economic variables flow together and that countries that are more advanced in terms of policy and institution building can effectively use foreign assistance as a tool to unlock development constraints are basically self-evident: getting development strategies to work is the only way to make rapid progress against poverty and that ultimately, only poor people themselves can choose best how to do it. From this perspective, it would be a mistake for policy emphasis to be placed on the conditions under which the developed countries will increase their lending effort rather than on the conditions under which developing countries will generate the greatest returns from their available resources. How poor countries build their institutions is a political decision – aid agencies cannot do it for them.

Corruption and Its Impact on Poverty
Although the social consequences of corruption may be most severe on the poor, the cost of corrupt activities to the society as a whole is high. Trust in government, or what is called "a culture of legality," is much lower and the resulting legal and administrative systems more inefficient where corruption is widespread. The most vivid and potentially the most lethal implication of this inefficient use of social investment is the neglect of both agriculture and edu-

cation. The most stunning evidence of this neglect is the very high level of mortality and malnutrition in the world's poor countries, living reminders of the millions of unnecessary deaths. Reconciling increased social and regional equity and the reduced concentration of income with growth that both improves material welfare and sustains substantial reductions in measured poverty is an overriding economic choice for poor countries.

Widespread corruption has plagued the developing world for many years. Its devastating effects are evident, reflecting in some cases what has been called a "development paradox." Most affected are the poor and the near-poor, whose limited resources are allocated on whims rather than needs. The poor, with their lack of political voice and social status, are victimized by the self-interested behavior of government employees, tax collectors, and other public officials, and are the losers not only in terms of extortion and bribery but also in terms of reduced access to good schools, medical facilities, and agricultural extension services.

Good Governance and Accountability

For the extreme poverty countries that exhibit these bad governance attributes, development strategies that emphasize the building of sustainable friendly institutions are thought to be the most effective. These might include advocating political decentralization, experimenting with checks, balances, and separation of powers, or creating or supporting non-governmental organizations and other institutions that enhance the transparency of policy-making, to name some well-known examples. By contrast, aid-financing of investments in these countries that do not address the problems of weak governance distinctly more often has poor outcomes.

The developing countries in which bad governance is most often cited as the key obstacle to social change in general, and poverty reduction in particular, are those with governments that are highly centralized, lack transparency, and fail to hold officials accountable. It is no surprise that good governance is least often a key problem in countries that are transitioning to democracy. In such transition countries, political liberalization and the rise of institutions that hold political leaders accountable can tip them toward adopting policies that otherwise serve the interests of the many rather than those of the elite. Meanwhile, of course, poor governance is often identified as the key obstacle to change when governments of any political stripe are not delivering social gains to their citizens. The challenges preventing citizens in these countries from holding leaders accountable seem to be confounded by weakly established institutions for state-citizens bargaining.

CHAPTER 7

Technological Innovations for Sustainable Developm

The living standards of the poor can be raised only when a sufficient level of public and private investment in human and physical capital takes place - even in the face of the known market failures and the inevitable risks faced by the most vulnerable members of society. The goal of the global development community should not simply be to reduce the risk faced by the poor, but to facilitate the flow of resources to those sectors and groups that can most effectively use them and to foster those policies and institutions that promote sustainable growth.

At the core of the principles articulated in the United Nations Millennium Declaration is the recognition that all countries must contribute to the realization of shared international development goals and that enhanced international cooperation for development is vital. These principles recognize the close linkage between social and economic development and environmental sustainability. The principle is based on mutual acceptance of our responsibility to sustain the world's environmental system and of the benefits that flow from cooperation on international environmental issues. The principles focus on the establishment of a wide range of national and international institutions to further the implementation of all of these goals.

Information and Communication Technologies (ICTs)
They still remain too high in many parts of the world, even for these fairly low-cost solutions. More advanced programs, specifically intended as distance education programs using ICT, also exist, in which students are provided with a variety of programs that they can access in order to research and to learn. Few of these programs have been evaluated, and it is not absolutely clear from the evaluations whether the students, particularly in the primary educational years, would be better off receiving more routine teacher instruction, but the programs are often popular, and enable students and schools to access new teaching materials and resources.

Around the world, a large variety of imaginative schemes and programs are being implemented in remote areas, with remote access often provided through communication satellites. This trend in the use of ICT is likely to grow in the future, and while there are already some success stories, much remains to be done to secure the systemic and sustained use of ICTs within the rural development and poverty reduction context. The most common use of ICT in the rural development context is for education. Programs exist all around the world in which children, and even, in some cases, adults, are provided with access to the internet or distance learning programs in the form of proprietary course materials that have been produced by a recognized educational institution. The costs of such programs have been falling due to the easy availability of very low-power terminals and receivers and the greater amount of bandwidth available on satellites.

E-Government and Digital Services

The benefits of a totally virtual IDRC include: 24-hour global operations/seamless global coverage and presence in every time zone; seamless continuous learning and upgrading by linking IDRC with the global knowledge commons; a global information, e-learning and best practices reservoir available to all staff and clients; and better and cheaper support services. The risks of the push towards virtuality include insufficient attention to the potential costs (especially absent office learning) and built-in barriers to the development of working relationships and trust. The World Bank model (business-content in daily operations plus a global knowledge portal for knowledge-sharing and learning) might be more prudent in this regard. Both models are likely to co-evolve, but some choice of a primary model by the IDRC in 2000 may be necessary in order to take coordinated effective action.

By this model, all IDRC offices and knowledge workers would be resource networks, able to draw on e-learning tools, libraries, best practices as well as the best recent knowledge. By the same token, they would also be knowledge resources, available to the world, to network by e-mail, video conferencing, tele-conferencing, etc., and to work for and through a global knowledge commons. This model would transform the IDRC into a totally virtual organization, a distributed but co-integrated network of knowledge workers, information resources and knowledge management services, providing policy research and development solutions and services to clients, individuals, governments and civil society networks worldwide.

CHAPTER 8

Partnerships and Collaboration in Poverty Eradicat

The global partnership described in this chapter is the best investment the rich world can make in its own future. It is an inexpensive investment: most of the returns go to the poor, but the rich also benefit hugely from even the partial growth that is created by this investment. The investment is also likely to be a profitable one. Rich countries, with rapidly aging populations, are searching for profitable places to channel their savings. To date, we have mostly observed these private international financial flows bypassing the poorest parts of the world. Why not inject these flows directly into the world's most promising investment? Why not invest directly in "pro-energy" development? This is the essence of the policy conclusions of this book.

This book has argued that we have the tools to end extreme poverty. This final chapter has laid out a practical guide for a broad-based partnership for achieving that outcome. Three main steps in the strategy would be: (a) all societies should put in place the basic building blocks - quality education, basic health, safe water and sanitation, and adequate nutrition - for ending deprivation; (b) countries that act on these building blocks, such as through the public expenditure tools discussed here, should be given the financial assistance they will need to do so by donors, both multilateral and bilateral; and (c) poor countries themselves should push to take advantage of these opportunities and ensure that the productivity of their people is utilized fully.

Public-Private Partnerships

The government and any community conspire with the private sector, NGOs, and other regional or national enterprises to offer public services and produce goods. For instance, partnerships in health might be established with a hybrid healthcare network in the private sector plus private enterprise providing logistics and products. Funds would be provided for activities such as social marketing, management, demand generation, and investment in social franchises. These partnerships help legitimize private activities, hold entrepreneurs and civil society participants accountable, and further policy reforms. Public resources are leveraged, and some of the benefits of privatization can be passed on to the poorest through agreements between the private investors and NGOs or the communities involved.

Designing the most efficient and effective programs to end poverty is complex. Governments, the public sector, and official development agencies have a large role to play in achieving successful outcomes. But today, the nature of the partnership between governments and international financial agencies has been changing. An alternative approach has proven successful. This approach starts with the proposition that the best programs to alleviate poverty are those that mobilize and empower the poor.

International Aid and Development Assistance

The increase in the number of available aid channels has come about in response to the waxing and waning of public opinion in the donor countries, in search of something tangible that can be done in support of "sustainable development". These channels include the international aid agencies (IAA's), the regional development banks, the UN specialized agencies (UNDP, FAO, WHO, etc.), UN Operations, the World Bank, national public development agencies in donor countries, international nongovernmental organizations (NGO's), and multinational corporations (MNC's). The proliferation of channels is in response to the search for politically acceptable projects that can be carried out with the requisite collateral benefits in terms of cash flow, jobs, training, technology transfer, and export opportunities. But the "search-for-collateral-benefits" at the country level exacerbates the country problems.

There is a widespread feeling in the donor community and in the developing countries that present systems of aid and international assistance are not working well, not alleviating poverty, and not effectively channeling funds toward high-priority programs. The problem of aid is not that the donor countries are making it difficult for the World Bank, the regional development banks, and other aid agencies to absorb their financial support through their concessional loan programs. The problem that is confronted by those institutions which disburse grant aid is that there are few highly effective channels for delivering technical and financial aid to a few countries, which in turn can be effective mechanisms for carrying out the best programs for poverty reduction.

CHAPTER 9

Monitoring and Evaluation of Poverty Reduction Pro

Processes of evaluation of potential interventions are understood to have four distinct attributes: (a) attribution and additionality, in which analysts attempt to identify the proportion of costs and benefits that can be linked directly to a specific intervention; (b) consistency and comparability, which try to make the data and the analysis comparable across different donors and countries; (c) effectiveness, the focus on results, cost effectiveness, and efficiency of potential poverty interventions; and (d) the likely significance of market or intervention imperfections on the poverty reduction potential of the intervention.

Assessing the impact of poverty reduction programs is an essential task for policy making. Without careful attention to process and effectiveness, such programs can easily become personality monuments, operations that consume large amounts of government and donor budgetary resources, but contribute little to aggregate poverty reduction. The process of evaluation attempts to compare the costs and benefits of poverty interventions, in both their financial and nonfinancial forms, all evaluated, where possible, from the perspective of the beneficiaries of the intervention. The identified costs and benefits should include not only the costs of implementing a program to completion, but also the costs to the beneficiaries themselves, including any assets that are lost, possibly irretrievably, in the implementation of a program.

Indicators and Metrics for Assessing Impact

Recently, the struggle to reduce extreme poverty became more codified when the world adopted the international development goal, or in other words, the Millennium Development Goal of reducing the percentage of people living in extreme poverty by one half between 1990 and 2015. The international goal was also divided into time-based national goals, and a reporting system was set up, followed by extensive comparison, benchmarking, and agreements for resource allocation. The result is that despite the appropriateness of the goal, the international debate among development practitioners about proposals, policies, and strategies to significantly reduce global poverty in the medium and long-term has yielded relatively few specifics and there has been insufficient attention as to what poverty reduction could and should mean. For example, how will the successful end of global poverty be understood?

How will the successful end of global poverty be understood? This is not a philosophical question, or not only a philosophical one, but also a question of how to assess whether the end of poverty has succeeded according to policies and practical observations. Success is not only a desired outcome, but also a response to the task of budgeting financial resources, evaluating investment, and comparing different approaches to solving the challenge of finding ways to raise the living conditions of the poor of the world. The answer will provide guidance to national, local, and international organizations and will improve coordination, monitoring, and evaluation during the design and implementation of policies and strategies for poverty reduction.

Case Studies and Best Practices

In particular, we have attempted to show how the East Asian tigers, Taiwan, and Korea, and more recently Indonesia, Malaysia, and Vietnam, have been able to incorporate into their growth strategies large segments of their populations that were at an early moment very poor or lived in subsistence agriculture with poorly paid informal urban labor that barely performed the most basic and generally non-creative jobs. We have been able to study in detail the case of the excess surplus labor of the countryside and the so-called oriental despotism of some pre-industrial societies, as well as the variety of incentive mechanisms to encourage the formation of a set of productive workers interested in the survival of the modern state.

There are many examples of countries, regions, and production systems that have significantly reduced or even managed to escape from poverty traps. We have analyzed in this chapter several of these cases, from the historical experiences of today's developed nations and those of the developing nations. Japan in the Meiji Restoration, 1868-1888, Taiwan and Korea in the post-1945 period, and China since 1978. Turning to the developing nations, we have pointed out how in the 1960-1990 period Indonesia went from being the developing country with the most unequal income distribution to being the most equal, and South Korea, modern Turkey, Thailand, and Vietnam have been able to continue growing fast in very diverse world historical periods and to also reduce inequality.

CHAPTER 10

Conclusion and Future Outlook

The rich countries and the world development agencies are constrained in the way they must approach the elimination of poverty. There is only so much that can be financed either via increased aid or difficult trade policies. International aid can be well used in many practical, near-term ways, amongst them in financing the many pilot projects needed, in general building local capacity as one approach, evaluating better other options, and providing the public infrastructure and policy framework necessary for development. These are serious constraints, but in principle, they should long since have been overcome in concert with an alignment of self-interest. For the final unjust indignity of global poverty is that the dogs of war, of whom President Eisenhower spoke, also suffer mightily, and feeding the dogs of war through foreign aid is a competitive spend of staggering magnitude. It's just that we finance it in order to destroy this food as quickly as possible.

The author begins this conclusion by emphasizing the unique nature of the problem of global poverty. Nearly half of the world's population still lives in dire poverty. Average income in an immensely productive modern economy can be 400 times higher than in a central African subsistence farming village. Many of the world's poor suffer from diseases that none of their contemporaries in richer countries have known for generations. They are illiterate and, for those unlucky enough to survive, opportunity and power are vanishingly small. Yet, the loss of them is within the grasp of the rich countries. Only an amount of money slightly greater than that spent by their government on foreign aid, or by society on champagne and cigars. Stated in this way, the paucity of the solution as well as the perversity of the inaction come into sharp focus.

Key Takeaways and Recommendations

To help poor countries move toward these goals, rich and other poor countries should strengthen their trade and other economic policies and significantly increase the aid they provide for means-tested programs in the poorest countries of four types: health, education, infrastructure, and direct income support. This aid could be provided on a year-to-year basis, it could be quarterly or annual, or, as the staff of the International Monetary Fund have been suggesting recently, a portion of the aid disbursements could be triggered by agreed steps by the recipient government. By providing incentives for ongoing policy improvements while signaling strong financial support for priority programs, this sort of arrangement is more likely to be successful.

It is time to commit to a new millennium development goals agenda. A nation's overarching goal should be to provide people everywhere, including their own citizens and foreign citizens living under their protection, with the opportunity to build a better life. These opportunities should include a good education, access to quality reproductive health; affordable, clean water, reliable sources of energy, and modern, efficient, and reliable infrastructure services, including telecommunications; security for personal and commercial property; a government that functions for the benefit of the governed; and the ability to benefit from the global economy.

Emerging Challenges and Opportunities

New technologies may result in many new benefits to the rural poor. Farmers in many environments, for example, will benefit from increased yields, and consumers will benefit from higher food quality. Genetic engineering, biotechnology, and other frontier technologies offer a variety of new applications in food, including fruits and vegetables, bio-fertilizers, pesticides, bio-remediation, medicines, and bio-insecticides, among others. These applications offer an expanded market for the small farmer, especially in areas where marginal technologies have been the barriers to the inclusion of small farmer participation in new agricultural markets.

Economic development through less expensive, capital-intensive, labor-intensive technologies will have a variety of effects, challenges, and opportunities. Seventy percent of the world's poor are in agriculture. New technologies may displace or greatly disadvantage the rural poor if they are capital intensive, land or water intensive, or highly dependent on purchased inputs. Intellectual property rights, which are important in stimulating research on new technologies, may be highly concentrated and thus disadvantage the poor. They also may restrict the spread and use of new technology if individual control of the use of new varieties results in excessive royalties, monopoly pricing, or restrictions on subsequent breeding by users.